Republic of Parts

© 2004 Stephanie Maricevic

Acknowledgements:
Several of these poems have been previously published in *The Antigonish Review*, *Descant*, *Event*, and *some stuff on canadian spoken word & indie publishing*, Joe Blades, editor (Montreal: National Campus and Community Radio Association/ l'Association nationale des radios étudiantes et communautaires, 2004).

Judges for the 2004 Poets' Corner Award: Denise DeMoura, Lorri Neilsen Glenn.
Cover: photo of the author's great-grandparents (1920s); kilim/carpet from the collection of the author.
Author photo by Judith Plessis.
Design and in-house editing by the publisher, Joe Blades.
Printed and bound in Canada by Sentinel Printing, Yarmouth NS.

No part of this publication may be reproduced, stored in a retrieval system or transmitted, in any form or by any means, without the prior written permission of the publisher or, in the case of photocopying or other reprographic copying, a licence from Access Copyright (Canadian Copyright Licencing Agency), 1900-One Yonge St, Toronto ON M5E 1E5. Tel 416 868-1620, 1-800-893-5777, fax 416 868-1621, admin@accesscopyright.ca   www.accesscopyright.ca

Broken Jaw Press acknowledges the support of the Canada Council for the Arts and the New Brunswick Culture and Sport Secretariat-Arts Development Branch.

Broken Jaw Press Inc.
Box 596 Stn A
Fredericton NB E3B 5A6
Canada
www.brokenjaw.com
jblades@brokenjaw.com
tel / fax 506 454-5127

BS Poetry Society
Box 596 Stn A
Fredericton NB E3B 5A6
Canada

Library and Archives Canada Cataloguing in Publication

Maricevic, Stephanie, 1969-
    Republic of parts / Stephanie Maricevic.

Poems.
Co-published by BS Poetry Society.
ISBN 1-55391-025-7

    1. Croatia--Poetry. I. BS Poetry Society. II. Title.

PS8626.A753R46 2004   C811'.6   C2004-904299-8

Republic of Parts

Stephanie Maricevic

Fredericton • Canada

Republic of Parts

Abroad
Blue Hands 8
Pašman Island 9
Čilipi: Conjectures of Buying a Rug 10
   Čilipi I, The Rug Afterwards 10
   Čilipi III, Olives 11
   Čilipi III, Oleander 12
   Čilipi IV, Dances 13
   Čilipi V, What *Baka* Might Have Thought 14
   Čilipi VI, Trta-Mrta Crazy 15
   Čilipi VII, Finale 16
Naasif's Dance 17
War Fragments 18
Dubrovnik Reincarnation 19
Gypsies in Josip ban Jelačić Square, Zagreb 1990 20
Mistral of Komolac 22
The Dream of Molunat 23
Wedding Preparation 24
The Venetians of St. Jacov's Cathedral, Šibenik 26
Survival 28
Adriatic Siesta 29
The Sea as a Rectangle 30
Train Station 31

At Home
Grandmother's Rituals 34
Bargaining 35
The Bulemic 36
Inheritance 37
Boat Ride on the Cunard 38
Vitals 39
Divorcing the Dog 40
Elsie's Dying 41
What We Know 42

Love is for Fishes 43
Bat Tree Opus 44
Keeping Score 47
Empty Spaces 49
Learning to Dance 50
You Needed a Jacket 51
After an Argument 52
Long Distance 53

Our Unwitting Slavs
Immigrant Job 56
As We Strolled Down Hastings Street by Woodwards'
 Christmas Displays 58
Two Famous Poets and a Car 59
Albert William 60
Eve's Truths 61
Funeral 62
The Cards Never Lie 63
Breakfast is Primal 65
The Real Words are in Paris 66
Art Deco 68
Mirage 69
Tropical Itch at the Moana 70
Variations of Bliss 71
The Heroine of Want 72
Peppers as a Metaphor for Everyday Life 73
Intact 74
Artifacts 75
Lessons 76
An Up-Ending 77

Abroad

Blue Hands

I met my grandmother
when I was sixteen, listened
to thick-tongued
blood syllables
and watched hands
flutter against the blue
walls of her flat.

She pressed holy gold
kissed by a Bosnian Pope
into my burning atheist's
hands. Filthy fingers,
saliva traces, etched;
small crosses tattooed
my lifeline.

She cupped my hands
to trace a resemblance, untangle
a pulse, but found only intimations
of a soul: blue, transparent.

She sewed me a dress
of seamless blue,
now ghosts flutter close
against the skin, threads
scroll blue tattoos.

Pašman Island

On Pašman Otok we walked up
the hills to the old town
in late afternoon when even the dogs
were asleep, their ears twitching
to the hum of cicadas.

The old bones at the cemetery
heard our foreign tones and rolled
over in their crypts, we heard them
sigh as we approached in our sandals,
the city echoing in our toes.

At the bar we ate fried *girice* with raw
red onions, the small fish eaten whole
and washed down with cold beer.

Nothing had changed in six hundred
years, a widow washed
her shawl in a basin
and flung it on the stone wall
around her garden.

She didn't even look up
no one ever looked at us
as they sat in the shade and drank
white wine from tall glasses
for six hundred years.

Čilipi: Conjectures of Buying a Rug

Čilipi I, The Rug Afterwards

In Čilipi she bought a rug the boy didn't know about because he was busy talking to that man with the attraction to old Italian motorcycles, she forgets the name and she won't ask him because he'll say not *just* Italian but a special kind and *tsk-tsk* at her woman's ignorance but it's not *woman's* it's just they were buying a rug that day and he was angry.

It was hot in the Citröen with the Austrian plates and a dead dog was lying on the centre line and she is sure she said, *we are all thirsty*, when the boy whined and kicked the back of her seat again. The father, the driver, didn't say anything, just gripped the wheel in his fists, glaring into the morning sun.

Now it's on the floor and he tells everyone the story of Čilipi and what a beautiful pattern of red and gold crosses and no one remembers anything about Gino or his motorcycle.

Čilipi II, Olives

That was the day when we met the man with the dusty wine glasses.

When we stopped the car in Čilipi there were only cicadas and unripe olives on the ground so we lay down under a lemon tree. When they got home the women watched while the men pulled their moustaches. First it was *kava* in little Turkish cups but you shook your head even thugh I could taste oily coffee roiling in my throat so they brought out the Plavac and Gino marched across the street and brought back wine glasses, perfectly etched roses intertwined with whorls of fingerprints on the rims.

When the boy brought out the guitar and sang "Here Comes the Sun" we knew it was going to be all right as we ate hazelnut cake and haggled over the price of rugs. You thought they liked you because Gino let you ride his motorcycle down the road, but that was when the mother looked at my hands and pointed to Gino's house, sweeping her arm across the wide white of the Dinaric Alps. When you got back you picked an olive, put it in your mouth and spat it on the ground, the flesh hard green in the dust.

Čilipi III, Oleander

The mother was very proud of the boy singing in English. The daughter sat away from us on a stone. She didn't talk or sing. The boy was like his mother, the boy was his mother many times that afternoon and no one could touch him.

I forgot to mention the oleander. I sat on the bench beside the tree and it was sweet; the salt in the breeze licked the petals. The old *baka* was dreaming in her chair, her gnarled hands gripped the wicker.

This man, not Gino, rubbed a dog with his feet: the toenails were long and black with grit — we could truly see the dog with its little legs and long underbelly. The dog's toes were as black as the man's.

The *baka* and daughter didn't appear to be needed although that could change very quickly.

Čilipi IV, Dances

The *baka*'s hands were claws on her lap. Hands that had woven St. Stephen in gold and red, a small cross embossed on his cassock, hands that wove maids with wide faces squinting against the sun, always the sun in this country of red wine and blood spilled on stone. She smelled of garlic and cloves and wet lamb's wool. There was something else too — the must of fatigue in her marrow.

The *baka* dreamed in a wicker chair and everything was old but her hair of pale gold in a loose chignon. She mewed softly in her sleep, maybe she was remembering when her hair was tressed, swirling around her head as she danced the Kolo like a gypsy around the fire. In the distance the scream of a stuck boar being hunted through the black pines.

Čilipi V, What *Baka* Might Have Thought

She put on her best dress when she saw the Canadians coming. They thought she was asleep when they knocked, but she was buttoning the rose-coloured dress, the one she wore on Sundays with the lace filigree on the hem. At the table, the *baka* saw the girl was restless as she watched the flies settle on the cake and she kept trying to shoo them away with her hand, but it was no good — too many flies and they had been there longer. The girl was only there for a moment, although she ate the cake as the family watched her take each small bite and swallow slowly, her eyes always on the mountains. The girl's father was one of them, he popped whole pieces of cake between his white teeth as he spoke of swimming in a cave where eels lived. The girl belonged to the father with her laughing dimples, not the young man. The young man though, the bearded stranger, was different. He liked the motorcycles and the *baka* couldn't recognize the camber of his language, even when he wasn't talking. She decided then he would never understand the flies belonging to certain houses only and the spot where the sun hit the karst just before dark.

Čilipi VI, Trta-Mrta Crazy

Gino's motorcycle gleamed in the street, the chrome spokes wiped down with a muslin cloth. He had been alone for a long time, since before the war when he was a waiter at the Hotel Adriatic and perfumed women flashed their smiles against the bleached white of his uniform. He never minded until he was drafted and wore a uniform for so many days and nights in the Bosnian hills, chafing the underside of his arms, epaulettes hanging past his shoulder blades, cuffs frayed and spattered with blood.

Now the motorcycles roar up and down the roads of Čilipi past the restaurant, Trta-Mrta, crazy upside down, and no one talks to helmets, he doesn't have to speak at all, just listen to the roar of the world through padded ears. Even when the helmet's off, sound is muffled and when his brother speaks to him, the words are under water. He repeats *trta-mrta* in his sleep clutching his balls, soft and hot against the sheet. Gino is underwater and his own voice is thick with drowning.

Čilipi VII, Finale

The Canadians are still in Čilipi every time they sit on the rug.

They climbed into the borrowed Citröen with the Austrian plates;
the girl worried aloud about the border guard at Herzegovina —
what would they do if the guards spoke to them in German? The boy
was the only one who laughed when they drove off, he tried to make
a joke of the day, to snipe at the girl for paying so much for the rug
but the girl just looked away out the dirty window to the hills.

They went swimming again, found a beach along the hot road,
maybe they stopped and swam in the bay at Hotel Babin Cook,
maybe they went to the cave and the girl shivered in the sea — she
hadn't known the eels were real. They thought they were untouched
that day, even though they bought the rug, scratchy and new and
stuffed in the trunk, rolled up beside the beach towels. They only
found out later, after they left that country — like the small red
crosses woven into the rug — the imprint was deeper.

Naasif's Dance

Back of the bus, he sits alone,
long legs swing, cross & uncross.
He will study ballroom dance, this
Naasif, this twenty-one-year-old,
I vill fight for my country.

I want to ask if his daddy told him
how to carry an AK-47 and do the tango.
Naasif with his slender hands offers an orange,
the knife wittles the peel gently and precisely,
he should be an orange surgeon and not a soldier.

Naasif loves the English waltz
and I want my body pressed
against the length of him,
we would waltz to the rhythm
of a diesel engine rolling over potholes.

Naasif strides off the bus, suitcase
caressed in his long arms,
in the street lamp, long leg
shadows swing, cross & uncross,
the bus moves on in the night.

War Fragments

                        you cannot imagine walking
            in Petrinja   you cannot imagine walking
              the street glass and boarded windows
                   Grass springs up, small blades
                        in hot sidewalk
                   The butcher shop, bakery —
                  bread & blood hardened together
                   The road is painted   carefully
               white   lines for the cars that never stop
here. Euro hair salon's door swings   open
             when the trucks drive by, inside hair dryer
             monoliths: twisted wires and plastic heads
                where Serbian stylists once smoked
                   Rothmans and curled their hair
                     There are no   sparrows
                             singing
     in the trees   there are no lindens

Dubrovnik Reincarnation

You stood in the square
and told us, thousands of years before
you were a Roman soldier
and when we opened our eyes
your barrel-chest heaved
with the weight of carrying
sword and shield.

We marched along the ramparts
in the sun and you didn't break your stance
until some German tourists disturbed
the reverie with their quick laughter.

You were stately that day
and even speaking was irrelevant
to the terrain and your new conception.

You scoffed when we brought
it up years later and couldn't recall
your tears when you stood alone
witnessing your death in battle with the Illyrians
over and over.

Gypsies in Josip ban Jelačić Square, Zagreb 1990

In black patent leather women hurry along,
the men knock back *rakia*
in the cafés lining the boulevard.
It is snowing and the pigeons fly
from roost to roost, unsettled
over hatted hair and newspapers. Every shop
window is bursting with goods: Turkish rugs,
votive candles sanctified by the bishop,
neapolitan wafers, rosehip jam and tea,
even though the British Consulate has closed,
Zatvoren/Fermé says the sign as a guard
paces the gates.

I want to return my books to the consulate library,
this hardcover romance weighs on my arm
but there is no drop box, *zatvoren*.
Yet it is December 26th, St. Stephen's Day
and the Orient Express Café
is open. They serve the best cappuccino
in the city and patrons line the mahogany bar,
only the gleam of gold teeth reflected
in the chrome espresso machine
and an occasional garlic sausage
in a sack distorts the quiet elegance.

The snow falls faster now
the stones of the square slippery
as Josip ban Jelačić, freedom fighter
watches impassively from his marble horse
as the people below tread more carefully.

No one trips over the gypsies
crouched below the stone ledge;
the young mother, *babushka* on her head
with her perfectly formed boy
child, his dark hawk eyes scan
the crowd, slender stumps
where hands should be
as if they had been carefully placed
in the hand-cutter, the operator
calculating his measurements
with a slide rule, we'll just cut
to here, leave the arms.

A friend says the gypsies are the ones
with all the money.
They earn it from begging and other nefarious
dealings in corridors, rough hands
picking locks, long tresses against bare backs.
They live in the big houses, the friend tells me,
in the uptown, and I see them dancing
through a frosted windowpane
a glittering chandelier, thin
stumps unfettered from rags,
ghost hands playing the fiddle.

The square is emptying, the snow
falls thick and the pigeons coo
in the alcove above Zagreb…anka Bank.
Finally, the gypsy heaves herself up,
she has been sitting all day
on stone, her boy in her lap,
and she lifts him, one small foot
dangles as she walks,
his dark eyes follow the snow
over her shoulder.

Mistral of Komolac

Marinko's house in Komolac is full of him,
battened down with mosquito nets, shuttered
windows, his old man's shuffling ways, evening
coughs close to the bathroom. Sometimes he calls
to his wife in her crypt late at night in a dream
while the mistral blows through the transom
charming his memory, making him young
again with his brother in the hills above the town
overlooking the river where he fished with a string
on the end of a stick when he was seven.
Now he is seven again and they are hunting
boar with father's gun, will he be the one
to shoot, bare feet itching against pine needles?

Next door the ragged god of wind
resides in the stone wall of the mansion
that used to have a swimming pool, now full
of wild lavender, oregano, dill growing taller
than a child. Fragrances rush up
the grand staircase until the mistral
moves on to the old wine house, barrels
twelve feet high and just as wide, bullet
holes in their sides where wine gushed
out on the cobblestones, mixing with blood
because blood always spills with bullets.
It peeks through the boarded up door, sees
a skull in white and black, the diagram
of an exploding mine, remnants from the war.

This is the town where church bells still ring,
women dressed in black lace sing, mandarins
and lemons fall in the orchards and the cock
crows his longing all day. Marinko's house
pitches in the night while the wind makes ripples
on the water, river flowing to the sea.

The Dream of Molunat

In Molunat we found the only sea
with a sandy floor on that hard coast.

We drifted by a house built on rock,
French doors open to a patio, iron
chairs, a glass-topped table set for two.
I could live there, I decided, treading
water, waiting for the people
to arrive but they never did. No
one lived there, clearly.

A motorboat of teenage boys
steered too near our bobbing heads
and we looked up, awoke
out of the dream of Molunat
to see the lookout on the cliff, erected
during the war after the bombers came,
poured their cargo in this water.

We gazed down to the bottom,
small fish darted past our legs, to see
circles — swirls in the sand
that radiated outwards, under our plump
thighs undulating like clumps
of bleached seaweed above
the only sea with a soft bed.

Wedding Preparation

The pig squealed in the alley
as the knife nudged its pale skin
my breath soft on the feather pillow
as I lay reading to the whir
of a sewing machine next door,
a wedding dress for Maria.

Maria's wedding dress trembled
to the screams of the pig in the alley
as the knife slit through soft folds
and I blew slowly on the ticking of the pillow;
turning the page of my book I was reading
to the hum of the sewing machine next door.

Next door's sewing machine hummed
along the silk hem of Maria's wedding dress
but still the sound of the pig's cries in the alley
kept on with the sawing of the knife,
I held my breath against the pillow
gently turning the page of the book.

The book — I gave up trying to read
as next door's sewing machine ceased
and I could hear the rip of Maria's hemline;
in the alley the pig's squeal was softer, bleating
the flesh familiar now to the slant of steel
my breath releasing two feathers from the pillow.

The feathers wafted up in the air as I exhaled
and the book I was reading slipped down my stomach,
the sewing machine trundled briefly, then stopped
as Maria's wedding dress fell to the floor,
the air was hard, the pig was silent
while the knife ground against bone.

The bone snapped apart as the knife sliced,
the feathers floated to the floor,
my belly heavy with the spine of the book
as silk threaded through the eye of the needle
for Maria's wedding dress to be ready on Sunday
when the echoes of the pig in the alley
would be smothered in song.

The Venetians of St. Jacov's Cathedral, Šibenik

> *The cathedral is composed entirely of stone, and on the façade are 74 heads of 15th century Venetians, local citizens carved by the sculptor, Dalmatinac*

The weight of it all bearing down
on them is what they find
interminable, not the stony silence
or the tourists and saints, sisters
dusting them on Tuesday mornings.
It's the weight on their heads
with no neck and shoulders to bear it.

Carved into the façade, heads turned
toward each other, permanent
expression of surprise from the one
in the three-cornered hat —
   once I walked the streets here as a free man without ardour.
Now he is full of it, the desire
to leap out and touch the face beside him,
her hair in braids.
He has learned these things are difficult
without the body.
The woman never looks at the man
in his fancy hat, no. She is stretched,
her neck long and strong,
arterial vein bulges from all that work
in the fields picking olives.
Once she had feet that were wide,
heels split and hard from walking barefoot
on dry ground all day.

They watch tourists pass by, ice cream
dripping from their fingers, greedy tongues
flick ridges of pistachio and neopolitan.
   Why do they stare so, wonders the woman

mouth parched, and he tries to turn his head
to view her cleavage but he can't, he's stuck
in stone and can't quite see!
It's better this way, he thinks
   dreaming is better, she's probably got warts and sour lips
but she doesn't, she is
beautiful, stone suits her;
her profile was never so straight when she was alive.
The sculptor gave her a pointed nose
and she is constantly puzzled
by the haughty air of her nostrils.
The weight of it,
   what's the use of being a head —
thinks the man in the three-cornered hat,
   with no body to express my requirements?

   I'd rather be just a body,
the women knows, no head at all, just the body to tend the fields and
squat in the dust,
   I miss my stomach with its soft folds.

Survival

She pours *rakia* in small cups,
serves *smokva* — figs plucked
from the tree that morning,
fire followed with figs
the elixir forging a line down the stomach
to drown the worms infesting the intestines.

After *rakia*, the milk,
    I don't like milk, Baka.
I heard the story so many times, how her son
almost died in 1947, allergic to cow's milk
his body wracked with heaving. How
he was saved by a goat — full of calcium,
warm hairs from the udder.

I watch them eat, mother and son
suck marrow from bone
in unison, crunch the wing, wipe
up every morsel in the bowl
with thick slices of bread.

She collects drippings from the grill
and when I wash dishes I find bottles,
small vases, pomade tins packed with fat
rancid in the close air, and throw them out
when she isn't looking, guilty
of being alive.

After the war they would have killed for this,
sucked spoonfuls of lard for lunch.

Adriatic Siesta

The heat leaves us
bloated, unable to flick
even the wasps away from the plate
of smoked sausage and aubergines.

Children are the only movers
in this weather, their voices
muted in the humid air
as they call in the alley, bare feet
running over glass and grit.

The fig tree weeps fruit
and in this close space
I can hear the trickle
of sap ooze from its skin.

The sea is too bright today
it hurts the retinas, bounces off
cheekbones into hollows red
from sun in yesterday's swim.

No one sleeps in the evening,
night is for accordions and puffs of wind
from the shore, teasing us into life,
stringing us up for a few hours
of relief from the cycle of heat on stone,
salt and aquamarine.

The Sea as a Rectangle

At the Hotel Neptune, a rope
formed the border of the pool in the sea.
Nude sunbathers surveyed swimmers
in the rectangle below
while small black snakes slithered in rock
around browned feet.

The white of sunless asses peeked
through the waves, two half-moons
on the surface inside the strand,
open ocean on either side, open
to those who dared to duck
their heads and glide, buttocks
sliding under rope. But no one
did — the sunbathers drank
their mineral water and watched
from dark sunglasses
as the half-moons slid across
a cordoned sea.

Train Station

The leaves in August were turning, falling across the tracks of the station as we sat on the platform with our soft leather suitcases stuck to our thighs. We'd been warned of theft in public places, spaces where the air blew through our hair from the wrong direction and we clutched our cases tighter to our hips, our bodies changed where we didn't belong, even clothing bulged in new lines along our silhouettes. When the train came we were smaller in those seconds of waiting. We didn't need to examine our watches, our bones were clicking in our skins and we looked over at ourselves, shifting naked on the rail. Over and over we saw the leaves on the track flutter upwards, now crumble in pieces, now still as we waited, breathing the air of the place, not realizing in this careful attendance we were already altered; the suitcases soft against our thighs, stroked our transformation.

At Home

Grandmother's Rituals

Elsie Jean singed
the hair off her forearms
over the gas stove every morning
before anyone else got up
until no hair grew anymore,
only smooth skin, empty pores
where blond strands used to be.
She'd smoke a cigarette
and calmly hold her arm
over the flame, the reek
of hair quickly crackling and Players Light
mingled with coffee droplets on old lino.
She'd singe her hair and listen to the finches
bathing in a bucket on the porch.

Bargaining

My mother wears her worries on her wrists.

   They take shape, a small dot
   spreads until her doctor burns it off
   before I can read the rough scrawl.

I want to tell her
what really happened to the pearl
handled carving knife and the button shoes,
that I didn't lose her
amethyst ring down the bathroom sink.

I promise I'll make the tea right,
I'll pre-heat the pot and never
step on cracks.

The Bulemic

He couldn't eat alone
after his grandmother died.

They left him with a bowl of risotto,
little legs dangling from his chair,
shutters open to the garden and black
shadows gathered outside his Nona's bedroom.

The scent of the mimosa tree mingled with seafood
congealing in the bowl, his mother moaned
between the hard tap of his heels
against the wooden chair.

Now when he eats alone
he hears the moaning, chokes
down the cry, tries to swallow
his own silence.

Inheritance

My cousin and I hold the property
of our mothers' grudges close to our chests.
Mine got all the family photographs,
but his mother didn't invited her sister
to the wedding.

Hands clasped we carry a bolt
of the past in a mauve silk dress
given to the younger sister to wear
to her graduation, sweat stains
from the elder still in the sleeves.

It is a heavy weight we share,
an oak tallboy with secret
compartments, a sterling silver
flatware set, *Encyclopaedia Britannica*,
the 1942 edition: Hitler hailed as hero then.

   You —
my cousin's voice accuses
and my aunt speaks from his thin lips
and I become taller, older
though he is five years ahead of me.

In a minute I will chase him
with the broomstick up the attic stairs
and he will cut off my curls
with the kitchen shears,
snip-snip in the morning sun
behind the hedge.

An antique escritoire painted pale
green, two spoons, our grandfather's honour:
a Victory medal —
we await our portions.

Boat Ride on the Cunard

She bought her straw hat on the Suez Canal. She got off the ship, stepped lightly on the gangplank and picked the hat from a hawker's stall, twirled the brim in her fingertips and flipped it on her curls at a jaunty angle. After that the captain invited her to first class and every night she trooped up the stairs in her one good dress, always with a different set of beads flashing. Mornings were spent waiting, throwing frisbee on deck with the boys from second class, the ones she should have married, but didn't want — their starched collars and scuffed brogues.

In Singapore she bought a fan from a man in rags, overpaid her five coppers while the man in rags grinned his two-teeth smile. She walked the streets of Calcutta in her white gloves and straw hat, weaving daintily through the spice stalls, her twenty-five-year-old walk, balanced on the balls of her Mary Janes. She stopped and saw a snake charmer make a cobra dance, and clapped, her gloved hands thudding together against her bodice. In China she ate barbecued chicken feet, monkey brains, pigeon in coconut curry, bought silk pajamas softer than her one good dress and wore them to the officers' costume ball, straw hat on her head.

She learned to play bridge with a gentleman, tux musty smelling of cigars and hair pomade. She was quick and they won every round, the old playboy and the farm girl, every hand charmed.

When she came back she kept the hat in a box for fifty years, the black silk band never showed wear, she never took it out again, never travelled from the island, bringing up her babies with dreams of silk pajamas, strings of beads.

Vitals

In those days in Nelson they washed
once a week, the galvanized tub
filled to the rim with steaming water
hauled from the pot on the stove.
She taught her daughters
the rites of cleanliness — they always
washed their hands before dinner,
after tea with dark carbolic soap,
rough on their cheeks
before piling into the bed warm
from the brick their mother heated
in the stove and wrapped in newspaper.
They learned to wash
their vitals with a facecloth,
two sisters scrubbing the down
of underarms and thighs
before pulling on darned
wool stockings, girdles encasing
pale buttocks, small bellies.
She made them wear woolen vests
sewn from their father's old suits,
tweed chafing their chests
itchy and warm, they marched
down Carbonate Street holding hands
on the way to school, two
well-dressed woolen sausages, vitals
glowing below.

Divorcing the Dog

My dog's eyes knew before we did
that one day we would leave him
on the neighbours' front lawn, a gift
tied to their Japanese maple, a small black
ball huddled against fallen red leaves.
That one day my parents would tear out
their own eyes and hearts and dump them
weeping on our scarred kitchen table
where the elm tree scratched at the window
and we were never sure if it was the wind
or the dog at the door. There is always a tree
against a window, after seventeen years
an old elm at the glass and when it sways
in the wind I can hear the dog howl.

Elsie's Dying

Yellow oak leaves sweep
along floorboard splinters
on the front porch shaded
by forsythia branches,
in the corner, moths flit.

You shrouded yourself in red
brocade curtains veiled
against the east and children's shrieks,
open only to twilight seeping
through dust on bevelled glass.

You could see the holly tree,
but not the old green gage
plum tucked among cedar shadows
and the scarlet runners tangled
in string on the patio.

In every room traces of lavender
sachets and stale rosewater left
open in a long black bottle
on your night table. Eau de Tour Eiffel
mingled with old sweat.

All that August I sat in your white
Adirondack chair beside half-ripe plums.

What We Know

Here is the mantle piece,
the tulips in the vase with fresh water,
lampshades dusted, each pane of glass
wiped with a cloth. All the dishes
washed and dried and put away
on the shelf beside a marvel
of bottles and jars with never-expiring
expiry dates. In the bedroom the pillowcases
match the flowered bed skirt and the blankets
are folded and tucked in hospital corners.
We know: in this house
the curtains are ironed just so,
the pleats fall gradually
to the floor. In this house
drapes are drawn,
the front door never opens,
the dog always lolls on the mat
at the back, and the people,
they never leave,
they can never bear to leave.

Love is for Fishes

I didn't love you for your compassion
when you stopped for that man
and changed his tire on the highway in the storm.
It wasn't for your cheek bones either,
or the barrage of three-syllable words
coming from your straight white teeth.

It was the swimming,
or maybe because none
of the others could
— I'd watch them enter the sea,
pale arms flailing against salt and algae,
wind and tide, desperate to get back
to the weight of the earth pulling them down,
the need to breathe outweighing
the return to watery womb,
forgetting where they came from
I assumed.

But not you – you were fish
slicing the water, a dolphin
diving for a gold ring,
your words pleasing
three-syllable bubbles, teeth
effervescent white in the sun.

But on land you walked stolidly,
tail splicing into legs,
fins smacking the useless air.

Bat Tree Opus

I

There is a man playing the piano at the bottom of the stairs, his suit jacket worn, threads straining at the bulge of shoulder muscle. Cigarette smoke wafts up in the yellow light from the lamp on the walnut table. If you saw him undress, folding his clothes neatly on the chair, you'd know he'd been a boxer in the army from the discipline of his spine, small scars where leather gloves grazed his ribs.

He is playing Schumann's "Kinderszenen" for his daughter, Elizabeth, who listens with her ear against the banister, the rhythm of the ivories reverberating up through the wood. The younger sister too, the one with curls, listens and twirls her hair listlessly. She has already had her piece — "Baby Face" — she is serenaded every night, but it isn't fair. Elizabeth gets Schumann and she wants Schumann too. For now we have the music, Father, and two sisters in shortie nightgowns. The mother never figures in these scenes because she's always doing dishes or plucking the chicken or crying into muslin curtains, but not this mother, she's out back smoking on the lawn, watching the moon, waiting for the children to go to bed, waiting for her evening to begin.

II

They are at the cabin, Elizabeth, Baby and Mother. Father comes on weekends. They can see their house from across the lake — only at Six Mile and already so very far from town. The girls are planning — Elizabeth has all the plans, Baby wishes she had some but can't seem to think because she is so consumed with worrying about her sister's. Elizabeth, for her part, can't go anywhere without Baby: It has been decreed by Mother. She spends her time plotting her escape.

III

Midnight on the lake and the wind has come up; tiny waves lap the shore. It isn't really midnight, it's only 10:39, but this is what Elizabeth has told Baby, who believes her. It is midnight and they are walking towards the Bat Tree and Baby is afraid. Elizabeth is secretly gleeful, she's the one with the plans, so why not. The Bat Tree stands at least a hundred feet high above the lake, not far from the Byng Boys' Apple Orchard. The Byng Boys are mostly dead but the name stuck and that's the way it is in small towns. Elizabeth and Baby stand under the tree and they can see whitecaps on the lake when the moon comes out from the clouds. There's going to be a storm and there's nothing doing at the ol' Bat Tree so Baby grabs some dirt and throws it upwards and bats wake up screaming and Baby is screaming as screechy bat wings fly past her freshly washed curls, taking a swipe at her baby cheeks.

IV

Mother says it's a *chestnut* and if she ever catches them (meaning Elizabeth) going there again, she'll tell Father to bring the strap. Baby has Band-Aids on her face and likes to push her curls behind her ears when Mother is around. Baby has discovered that she can have her own plans and most of them involve inflicting her sister.

V

A culmination of lives. Father will die early, World War I mustard gas finally creeping up his lungs until he can't breathe and his heart gives out from the weight of carrying it all so deep inside.

They won't go back to the Bat Tree again. Every year it will bear glorious chestnuts plucked by the squirrels until young
Mr. Byng-Downie cuts her down to make a road for his new house in the hills.

Mother, in her dotage, will try to record family events on a tape recorder, but she is so embarrassed that all her descendants get to hear are fits of geriatric giggling in between her smoker's cough.

Schumann's opus will never be played for Baby, and this event will be a source of strife between the sisters for the rest of their lives when Baby, drunk at a dinner party, will insist that is *was* played for her, her alone.

Elizabeth will marry, have children. They won't grow up with a piano and this will bother her for a long time, but she'll be too preoccupied to do anything about it. Only on the occasional evening when she's in the garden sneaking a cigarette and the moon comes out, she'll hear the piano and smoke from far away.

Keeping Score

On Kootenay Lake I learned to hate
you in the canoe when you told me
you went fishing with your father
lots of times, plunking your bum
firmly on the plank seat.

There's gunge on the water,
I said and stopped paddling
to watch the dragonflies
lick algae off the green surface,
canoe drifting along the bank.

There's no such thing
as gunge, you said, rightly
and I took my paddle, hooked
the golden water, splashing
your bare shoulders.

I dared you to walk past the bats
in the chestnut tree at midnight,
made you walk up the old road
alone in a storm, lightning
and the threat of bears for company.

When we swam in the middle
of the lake I told you about the boy
who stepped off the shallows
at Willowpoint and was never seen
again though they dragged the bottom.

All that summer we reeled
off challenges in the dark,
searched for weakness in the line
of our conversations, strung
out across damp bunk beds.

It wasn't until I saw
I could make you afraid
the fishing didn't matter so much.

Empty Spaces

You have gone out and I am
reading Hemingway, your book
pretending that I hate every word.
You have gone and it's the first time
I've been alone in nine years and I can't hear
   yet, although a space opens
and I breathe into it,

my feet are sore and I'm too tired
to make dinner now, though I planned
to do your favourite, eggplant *parmigiana*.
The eggplant is too bitter and complicated.

I eat
bread and cheese. We used to call it pizza
when we couldn't afford to order one
there are many things to do: unwrap
a bar of soap, pick lint off your wool
sweater bought that time in Dublin,
cruise the aisles of London Drugs
for mint toothpicks.

I try to erase you
for five minutes and just be
someone else,
but I need more
time to remember how
to cook for one.

Learning to Dance

We stand like two chopsticks
   waiting for   the waltz   to start.
Two chopsticks rigid against smooth
floorboards, stiff elbows, unyielding hips.
Even if you could understand the verb, *gyrate*
your torso wouldn't comply, fused
from the knees up
in this Protestant stance.

Later I watch you clean a cornice, balance
one leg on a wobbly chair, an arm gently
coaxes the rag along narrow edges
stomach taut and long as you rise,
and still
you will not dance, feet firm
in concrete deliberations.

You Needed a Jacket

Square shoulders in conservative blue
as if it made you the company logo.
The sales clerk called it a blazer
and I pictured you blazing at lunch
in blue finery.

I picked it, plucked it from the rack
of Canadian wools but you wouldn't agree;
you wanted to work for this distinction in navy
as you had for the job, sorting through the classifieds
for six months before you got the call.

At Moore's the salesman tried to sell you
on Italian wool, black-and-grey houndstooth
on his superior knowledge of tycoon wear.
You were leary, not wanting to admit ignorance,
not knowing this breed of cloth was just a fancy name for check.

At the Bay you tried on the seven hundred dollar
double-breasted with crested brass buttons
that had to be altered until you saw the price,
and it was back to the jacket I'd glimpsed in approximate black,
the small sheen in exactly your size.

You said it wasn't conservative
and conjured the young dandy in a sea
of dark blue waistcoats, a buoy above
bellies and dandruffed shoulders
scowling as you admired the image in a three-way mirror.

When you got off the plane I endured the tacky jokes
from early breakfast meetings,
but heard nothing of the jacket, rumpled
in the rear and I knew then you'd worn it the whole time.

After an Argument

I see you through glass,
your voice a flat garble
I can hear, but can't decipher
the dialect of wrath.

Clear glass is the most difficult
to see through,
I can almost touch
but can't quite reach
through the pane.

I am left
standing on an empty street
outside a party of beautiful people
glimpsed through an open
curtain in a window.

They are transparent in the light,
the animation of their darting eyes,
lips so red in the fire of their discourse,
and the longing makes me cold,
pressed as I am against the glass.

Long Distance

I speak to my friend on the phone long distance to Ontario. I've never
been to Ontario and imagine quaint cottages on lakes, autumn leaves
fluttering from maple trees, boulevards with French names.
She is recently wedded, recently babied, recently moved to a small
town to become a house wife, moved to an affordable home
with neighbours you see in movies these days, never believing
they are real, Home Hardware hoses in their slack hands
they yack and water patches of lawn in the humid heat.
Her husband has a new job, works long hours, wasn't ready
to be a father, he says, but who is?

We used to speak, my friend and I, about everything — our sex
lives, for example, the scratchy lingerie
our spouses bought for us at Christmas,
knew solely by the amount of chocolate
we consumed whose PMS was worse.
I remember her dancing at a party once
face flushed, long hair wild
as she taught us all to rumba,
her young husband sitting
at the table watching her, only her.

Now we enunciate
graciously, speak
into the mouthpiece about
inconsequential items — a visit
from her mother expected,
the increase in the price
of honey due to the bee
disease, such a shame, I listen
to her sweet voice in my ear,
think of her husband,
watching.

Our Unwitting Slavs

Immigrant Job

Guiseppe worked the rail line
when he first came to Canada,
arriving in Halifax, first
view of the new world grey
rain and a roiling sea, the stink
of creosote and salt on the docks.

His job was loading rocks
on the ties beside the Poles
who didn't speak English
either, and the Irish, frustrated
because they were better
than this with their dubious
English the locals refused
to understand.

He borrowed money
for a taxi in Vancouver.
Bright yellow, black stripes along
the chassis, electric windows,
a radio, he came home
showed his wife and child,
went for a ride to Stanley Park
and it was beautiful that day,
Guiseppe's new taxi spotless and shiny,
smelling of new upholstery, hope
for the future, but already
grime was creeping into the edges,
in the corners that were too narrow
to clean with a cloth, where
it couldn't be seen, but palpable
just the same.

Joe's Taxi —
so many desperate people
sat within the plush black
clutching their grief
till it spilled out on the floor.
Would they have the money
to pay after leaving the husband,
only forty dollars in their pockets,
was there a hotel nearby and sorry
for the pain, for weeping as the dull rain
ran down the windows
and could they buy some cigarettes,
was it too late to stop
for a bottle?

It wasn't long before the taxi stank
of all that downtown bad
luck, not long before Joe
started to sag with his seats,
all the best intentions resting
on his tail bone. His wife got worn
out from waking up at five am to fix him
dinner before he went to bed,
and the child got tired of tiptoeing,
stomped around her room, not
long before Joe forgot what
he was working for and just kept on
going like windshield wipers
after the rain has stopped.

As We Strolled Down Hastings Street by Woodwards' Christmas Displays

I looked up to my mother
but it was someone else's hand
I held. Rudolph glared
at me with his red eyes as if to say
how could you have let go,
even for that instant?
Rudolph, orphaned reindeer — even he knew better.
What I couldn't understand was
how the hand felt the same,
this stranger with the same skin,
my skin flesh to flesh as we were, ambling
past the mannequins, crowds
of people busy with bags and boots
swishing in our path, their long coats
waves of dark wool undulating along
the sidewalk as I clung to my stranger.
I remember the shock of seeing
this smiling face that wanted to take me
home — her yellowed teeth, how her hand became
suddenly gnarled, cigarette-stained, hardened
as I gaped up at her. My mother
a few paces away on that dark sea
was looking at red dresses through the glass,
her leather boots with the broken zipper on one leg —
that leg, that one familiar beacon.
I knew then, right then, that she wasn't to be trusted fully.
My stranger held tight until she saw what my mother
saw and then she let go, disappeared in the lights
and when I looked back Rudolph wrinkled his nose —
safe, home free this time. But what if
I'd gone home with the other?

Two Famous Poets and a Car

I heard two poets talk
about driving in the rain,
how they used to love to ride, windows
rolled down to the wind,
to wet asphalt and rubber,
cedar stands whipping by, mile
after mile, hands holding the wheel
like caressing a shoulder
blade in the night.

The last of the bad road movie
stars, making pit stops for cheesies
and mountain dew, bare feet
curled against a faux mahogany dash,
the stick of bare leg against vinyl.
The thrill of going anywhere but home
because it's the last chance to be someone else,
and when are we going to get there?

One poet got up, read a poem
about arthritis, and I thought —
so this is what it's like
at the end of the road.

Albert William

Snap open his silver cigarette
case engraved *A.W.I.*,
fits nicely in my hand as it opens
and shuts. He would pull
it out calmly, coolly flip
a Dunhill in the corner of his crooked
mouth. No. He must
have smoked Gauloises, that's the only
cigarette to smoke under gas
lamps in a trench coat as April rain falls
gently on a felt fedora while deciding
which cabaret or café to dine in
in 1914.

I don't think his second
choice was the trenches
as mustard gas dallied with nicotine
for a second or two —
he snapped the case
open and shut to the shudder
of hand grenades. Only
the cigarette case
came back, snap.

Eve's Truths

EVERYONE KNOWS it wasn't like that.
  — Timothy Findley from *Not Wanted on the Voyage*

I would have done it all
over again, it was worth every juicy
morsel that snaked down my smooth
throat. That Adam's a bore,
I had to liven it up, couldn't you see
I mean, my *Gawd*
it was dull in that secret garden.
Don't believe a word they say,
it was a hole, let me tell you,
there were mice droppings
and hardly any water, all we had
to eat were boiled yams covered
in dust and every time one of my friends
from Olympus dropped by for a chat
all those petty Angels
would run and tell HIM
and Adam'd pout for days; jealous of Athena
for her golden bow (he wanted toys even then).
That was around the time Zeus got pregnant:
now there was a man ahead of his time.

Who would've thought we'd have to wear clothes?

The truth is
the truth *IS*,
everyone wants
the first
bite.

Funeral

I went to a funeral.
Two days later I was
old. Look
in the mirror,
my face is still
seated in the last
pew.

The Cards Never Lie

My father, logger
by day, gambled by night —
his evening profession scented with wood
chips and sweaty bunk beds.

In Trail he worked the railroad
with Italians from *Kampaloopsa*
and the Irish, *Nevar go down
a coal mine vid an Irish,
dey never look out for you,
    not even der own mudder.*

When he came home to our white picket fence
my mother called him a D.P.
every time he did something not up
to lace tablecloth snuff,
like when he said, *Shets man!*
his thick elbows obscene
in a rolled up lumberjack
shirt as he changed the tire
on my English grandmother's
Hillman.

*Nevar look away
nevar flinch
ven you turn ovar
da cards or look
at da dealer.
Be prepared to fight
vid da knife
in your boot alvays,
sleep in your pants
vid eye open.*

His best friends the Ace
of Spades and Red Jack,
da cards never lie.

How his daughter gurgled
at those gutteral words
of home that even he forgot
the meaning of.

Breakfast is Primal

Lolling, she asks in a slow drawl, precariously:
what would you like to eat at this very minute?

Breakfast, he says
sans hesitation,
breakfast is primal.
Any other meal is cognitive
(bacterial culture & wheat products),
she doesn't say.

Dinner is relished,
contemplated, *planned.*
Nibble passion carefully
between courses as red wine
lingers in fine breath, fire lips.

Rough, gobbled spoonfuls
dribbled on Formica is breakfast,
rushed grains, wood chips jammed
in gum lines, stale toothy daylight.

Morning is for warm beds
saturated in last night's
indulgences, release small odours
of onion skin in salty armpit:
her favourite meal.

Let's have breakfast, he says,
Man, I'm starved, pour cornflake
milk, six AM masticator.

Lolling, she listens
to the primate.

The Real Words are in Paris

The poetry you never write
when a seventy-year-old
woman floats along 4th Avenue
in her swish new hairdo, purple streaks
along her temples, roses tucked under her arm
as if she's going somewhere
important like on the next flight
to Paris in the spring.

The poetry you never write
on Sunday roads in the afternoon
when you're too hot and lost
and there's a kid selling lemonade
and it's the sweetest you've ever tasted
in the shade of a poplar, your dixie
cup filled with three pounds of sugar,
proud salesman beside you, clenched
buck in a small palm.

The poetry you never write
when it's minus fifteen and you pass
the man swathed in silk opera
scraps with elegant Lithium
eyes and realize later you did have
a loonie in your pocket.

The poetry you never write
after seeing your reflection in a shop
window in Vancouver rain;
you should be in a Woody
Allen movie you've got the right profile,
the right witty edge to your skin,
and you sit on a park bench in Strathcona
when a tall Chinese lady walks by
and she says, *you have a beautiful smile*
and you look at her and see
yourself in the dimple on her right cheek.

The poetry you never write
after fighting with your lover about herbal
tea and you're suddenly SO sure
it's over and drive home in a thunderstorm
while the radio plays Debussy's "Clair de Lune"
and you wonder why everything sounds
so much more romantic in French
and why you've never been
to Paris in the early spring.

Art Deco

I'm going to reside at O'Doul's
Piano bar, wear emerald
cut diamonds and apply lip paint
with my jewelled compact.
I want rose-coloured wallpaper
and palm-treed ladies lying
on *chaise-longues*, cigarette
holders held in their sulky lips.
Don't leave the martini cart
at the bar, bring it here
by my tortoiseshell mirror
while I bedeck my neck in coral
and lapis-lazuli. I'm waiting for Great,
the one called Gatsby to saunter along
in his panama hat and white linen.
We'll zigzag to Chicago
skyscrapers behind a Chinese
fan, the clink of black polished coffee
cups on marble tables. I'm told
gentlemen prefer blondes but I must ask
Mrs. Dalloway though she might be
on safari. Later this year I'll visit
Tut's tomb because I have a morbid
regard for antiquity, preferably
in geometric gold, but meanwhile
I'm going to linger here in 1922.

Mirage

Remember the *Bain du Soleil* woman?
Covered only in a silk cloth
as she reclined on a marble slab
beside la Côte d'Azure.
I imagined her in the evening: a black
velvet shift and spaghetti straps,
pearls around her throat
to emphasize the exquisite brown
of her tan, standing at the edge
of a Roulette table in Monte Carlo,
a dry martini with a twist
in her elegant fingers.

These days I see her
at Safeway, fluorescent lights
on mottled skin, a honeydew
in her hand.

Tropical Itch at the Moana

Clark Gable places his Panama
on the wrought iron table, crosses
his legs and orders a Tropical Itch, no ice
just Trinidian rum, a dash of lemon, orange
curacao and a small hint of whisky hidden
under a chunk of pineapple.

Tourists in tie-dyed saris, sequined bikini tops
come to see Clark, but find only water-
ed down drinks and half-starved
birds cheep-cheeping under iron
chairs, their stomachs
bloated with salty pretzels.

Singers in Victorian dresses
shuffle tired feet in narrow shoes
certain that when the music's over
they must take the long bus
ride across the island to steam
rice and taro for their children.

Clarkie doesn't care. He waits
till everyone leaves, the birds
twitch asleep in withered
Banyan trees, he sips his Itch,
tips his hat, and saunters back
into halcyon blue.

Variations of Bliss

This is a house with no love inside.
You might be fooled when you enter:
the photos stuck on the fridge
with the butterfly magnets bought
in Nevada and on Salt Spring,
the stack of birthday cards
in the stuffed drawer, the dried
daisy chain inside the book
of Neruda's love sonnets
from the Church Rummage Sale.
Don't be fooled: there is no
love inside this house. Look
closely in the fridge, no
Veuve Clicquot or even $8.50
Spanish Sparkling wine
only half-
rotten romaine and frozen rye bread
from the Austrian Bakery in Ladner.
In the bathtub, no
lovers caress backs in the steam
of sandlewood candlelight, not
with all those green rings and worn
out loofahs, candle ends, look
in the bedroom full of jumbled
clothes and dust; books piled
on too small night
tables, not
The Kama Sutra, no
massage oil beside the unmade
bed with rumpled red sheets and
plump pillows, no,
no love here.

The Heroine of Want

To live in a garret and sip champagne
with frozen lips, as icicles
drip from languid hips,
or to die of TB and be still
white in diaphanous lace,
embraced in my lover's lament.
Guiseppe di Stefano will sing me back to life,
his sweet tenor clings to the cage of the dove cote
as my jealous stepfather coos in the wings.
To have dueling suitors in tangerine bloomers
and silk stockings held up by velvet garters,
swords sing in the whipped air, light
as the single swan feather that drifts
from my Rapunzeled hair.
To be a Prima Donna
and sing an entire aria in staccato, or *andante*,
like Carmen, the gypsy witch desired
by scared Sevillian barbers.
To be a Japanese empress
encased in muslin embroidered
jade on a smoking lotus flower
oiled hair piled high, samurai
riding by on wild horses,
and my ministers sulk over the poor
trade in frankincense.

To be frozen lace
champagne
and frankincense.

Peppers as a Metaphor for Everyday Life
for Maria Sammarco

Peel a layer
with your fingernail
while idly watching tomato
sauce spatter the wall.

Put it in your mouth. A seed
lodges between your front teeth, hard
cayenne like the smell
of your mother's cracked
wooden salad bowl
she bought off
an Indian in Tofino
thirty years ago.

Look at your half
pep/per like
the inside of an old elbow
or a thigh after a swim,
cold and softly wet.

Stuff it with wild
rice and serve it to your husband
on English bone
china: it's shaped like the breast
of Cousin Georgina
who you always suspected
of wearing padded bras

or let it rot on the shelf
to remind you of an armpit
just after sex.

Intact

I

Think of how you'd feel
if you woke up and looked
down on the white sheet
and lifted up the covers to see
nothing but pink
dye, they didn't have
to cut you after all.

II

The calm as you lay
dying. Remember
the afterlife book? You knew
from the distension
of the stomach, first aid   first
sign of massive
internal hemorrhage
as blood filled
your ribcage. Every
breath   was.

III

It wasn't unpleasant. Your hair
felt smooth against a hypo-
allergenic pillow, the rough
polyester sheet was silk on your arm.
And distant voices like hearing
Emergency on TV from open
windows on a warm day
while you turned over
stones and listened
to a CPR performance.

Artifacts

Expired trophies for sale or rent
real gold bulb enhancers:
candlelit for moody swings
thumbnail games & retractable wings,
consider a clothes detacher.

Self-sharpening shampoo tiles
lint-defying blenders,
carpeted shocks that won't get piles
stoveless pots & oven fenders,
two for one radio dials.

Shoeless toes to keep by the door,
pillow necks that won't sleep in
cement blankets, lemon floors
scented bricks in fluted bins,
and tinned bonzai trees, sure to please.

Jello hats for windy days
soil-less doilies with small defects
aluminum foiled patio fleas,
scaled scarecrows to keep down pests
empty stairwells for the only guests.

Hanging basket soap detectors
spiders that sing Puccini arias,
used pumpkins at discount rates
candied glass that lives in crates,
and heartless apple pie, come buy

a small time miracle
candid blue and spherical,
come bargain for a tired face,
sell a smile for scraps of lace
to the discount lyric maker.

Lessons

I will be one of those
women who knit mittens
in blue and yellow rainbows.
I will understand when my daughter
won't dress her children in pink.
I will still knit
scarves in chocolate velveteen,
though I'll be chastised for sewing synthetics.
I'll bake cookies that no one will eat
because they contain animal products
and I'll buy three-ply white
toilet paper and use too much.
I will fold my plastic bags
neatly in a drawer, even though I shouldn't
use them, and polish my twenty-year-old calf
leather shoes. I will not
admonish my daughter when her kids
play with my pewter teaspoon set
and drop
them down the heating vent — *they were only
playing, they're only kids, it's only things
mother — I'll buy you new spoons* — I
will hold my silence close, careful
not to break anything.

An Up-Ending

Poets are always on the lookout for those crucial moments

under a flowering forsythia as their lover leaves them for something less literary, someone less prone to words, someone who *does*, isn't looking to record it.

Give them heartbreak hotel, lonely street, an Elvis impersonator staggering across a stage after the audience has left,

give them aging beauty queens with sad eyes caked in violet eyeshadow, but only violet,

give them a small black spider with one crushed leg, inching across a railing on the 24th floor,

give them estranged families
and strange families
who only speak when the moon is full,

give them a three-legged dog
without a collar right now,
huddled under a rusted car,

give them two drops left in a Dewar's bottle, though half-full would be more appreciated,

give them that song heard on the radio late at night, heard only once, but never forgotten, haunting them till the day they die,

they want it played at their funeral but no one can play it because they don't recall the name.

Give them coconut carved in the shape of a rose, but don't give them a rose for goodness' sake.

Give them Romeo and Juliet but call it something else entirely
and set in 1930s America during the Depression, if possible.

Give them two people talking in a foreign language
with hand gesticulations and dark espresso, no milky concoctions.

Give them an underdog, especially one who had a cruel teacher,
but don't use stepmothers, they make passé villains these days.

Give them a hero, better yet a heroine, make it a stepmother
with wicked stepchildren who want to eat her all up.

Give them cheerfully effeminate construction
workers hammering away in the winter,

give them fireworks on a summer night, fresh-cut
grass (grass can never be a cliché — it smells of perfect nostalgia),

Give them an old woman at a pub drinking Guinness
in her war medals on VE Day, preferably with a bulbous nose.

Give them trees, poets need a lot of trees,
or a nice piece of glass, stained if possible in vermilion,

give them a Japanese painting and a tea ceremony or perhaps
just a handmade clay teapot with jasmine, steeped for exactly three
minutes.

Heck, anything hand done, except macramé,
only if there's nothing else available, but don't

give them anything made of plastic, they might
put it in their mouths, although you

can drive them by landfills, especially
with one-legged seagulls and Kermode bears foraging.

Give them a sunset, but not in gold,
make it green, and make the sky crimson,

give them a grapefruit half-peeled and they'll write some pithy witticism,
or not, they might just eat that grapefruit, it depends where they got
their last meal.

A Selection of Our Titles in Print

Poets' Corner Award winners
2004   *Republic of Parts* (Stephanie Maricevic) poetry, 1-55391-025-7
2003   *All the Perfect Disguises* (Lorri Neilsen Glenn) poetry, 1-55391-010-9
2002   *Peppermint Night* (Vanna Tessier) poetry, 1-896647-83-9
2000   *Starting from Promise* (Lorne Dufour) poetry, 1-896647-52-9
1999   *Tales for an Urban Sky* (Alice Major) poetry, 1-896647-11-1

A Fredericton Alphabet (John Leroux) photos, architecture, ISBN 1-896647-77-4
Antimatter (Hugh Hazelton) poetry, 1-896647-98-7
Avoidance Tactics (Sky Gilbert) drama, 1-896647-50-2
Break the Silence (Denise DeMoura) poetry, 1-896647-87-1
Crossroads Cant (Grace, Seabrook, Shafiq, Shin. Joe Blades, editor) poetry, 0-921411-48-0
Cuerpo amado / Beloved Body (Nela Rio; Hugh Hazelton, translator) poetry, 1-896647-81-2
Day of the Dog-tooth Violets (Christina Kilbourne) short fiction, 1-896647-44-8
During Nights That Undress Other Nights / En las noches que desvisten otras noches (Nela Rio; Elizabeth Gamble Miller, translator) poetry, 1-55391-008-7
Garden of the Gods (Dina Desveaux) novel, 1-55391-016-4
Great Lakes logia (Joe Blades, editor) art & writing anthology, 1-896647-70-7
Groundswell: the best of above/ground press, 1993-2003 (rob mclennan, ed.), 1-55391-012-5
Herbarium of Souls (Vladimir Tasić) short fiction, 0-921411-72-3
Jive Talk: George Fetherling in Interviews and Documents (Joe Blades, ed.), 1-896647-54-5
Mangoes on the Maple Tree (Uma Parameswaran) fiction, 1-896647-79-0
Manitoba highway map (rob mclennan) poetry, 0-921411-89-8
Memories of Sandy Point, St George's Bay, Newfoundland (Phyllis Pieroway), social history, 1-55391-029-X
Maiden Voyages (Scott Burke, editor) drama, 1-55391-023-0
Paper Hotel (rob mclennan) poetry, 1-55391-004-4
Reader Be Thou Also Ready (Robert James) fiction, 1-896647-26-X
resume drowning (Jon Paul Fiorentino) poetry, 1-896647-94-4
Shadowy:Technicians: New Ottawa Poets (rob mclennan, editor), poetry, 0-921411-71-5
Song of the Vulgar Starling (Eric Miller) poetry, 0-921411-93-6
Speaking Through Jagged Rock (Connie Fife) poetry, 0-921411-99-5
Sunset (Pablo Urbanyi; Hugh Hazelton, translator) fiction, 1-55391-014-1
Sustaining the Gaze / Sosteniendo la mirada / Soutenant le regard (Brian Atkinson, Nela Rio; Elizabeth Gamble Miller, Jill Valery, translators) photo essay, poetry, 1-55391-028-1
Sweet Mother Prophesy (Andrew Titus) fiction, 1-55391-002-8
The Longest Winter (Julie Doiron, Ian Roy) photos, short fiction, 0-921411-95-2
The Robbie Burns Revival & Other Stories (Cecilia Kennedy) short fiction, 1-55391-024-9
The Space of Light / El espacio de la luz (Nela Rio; Elizabeth Gamble Miller editor & translator) short fiction and poetry, 1-55391-020-6
This Day Full of Promise (Michael Dennis) poetry, 1-896647-48-0
The Sweet Smell of Mother's Milk-Wet Bodice (Uma Parameswaran) fiction, 1-896647-72-3
The Yoko Ono Project (Jean Yoon) drama, 1-55391-001-X
Túnel de proa verde / Tunnel of the Green Prow (Nela Rio; Hugh Hazelton, trans.) poetry, 1-896647-10-3
What Was Always Hers (Uma Parameswaran) short fiction, 1-896647-12-X

www.brokenjaw.com hosts our current catalogue, submissions guidelines, manuscript award competitions, booktrade sales representation and distribution information. Directly from us, all individual orders must be prepaid. All Canadian orders must add 7% GST/HST (CCRA Number: 892667403RT0001). Broken Jaw Press Inc., Box 596 Stn A, Fredericton NB E3B 5A6, Canada.